AMERICA'S MOST WANTED

Public Enemy Number One:
"PRETTY BOY" FLOYD

Written by:
Sue L. Hamilton

Published by Abdo & Daughters, 6537 Cecilia Circle, Bloomington, Minnesota 55435

Library bound edition distributed by Rockbottom Books, Pentagon Tower, P.O. Box 36036, Minneapolis, Minnesota 55435

Library of Congress Number: 89-084923   ISBN: 0-939179-63-6

Cover Photos by: Bettmann Archive
Inside Photos by: Bettmann Archive

Edited by: John C. Hamilton

FORWARD

March 11,1930

"Look behind us!" said bank robber Tom Bradley, turning around in the back seat of the car.

"A cop," muttered Jack Atkins.

"We gotta' put some distance between us," said Charlie "Pretty Boy" Floyd. The trio had robbed a bank in the small town of Sylvania, Ohio. Now headed for their hideout in Akron, they had just driven inside the city limits when they ran a red light. Patrolman Harlan F. Manes gave chase. His siren blaring fiercely, the traffic cop motioned to them.

"Pull over!" yelled Manes. "Pull..."

Suddenly, the back window of the car shattered. The cop watched in shocked silence as a gun pointed out through the broken glass and began firing. The roar of the blasts drowned out the siren's blare. It was the last sound Manes would ever hear. The policeman was blown across the road, his body riddled with bullets.

Inside the car, Bradley yelled, "Got him!" Suddenly, the car lost control. Swerving back and forth, it smashed into a telephone pole, trapping the three bank robbers inside. A few minutes later, police arrived at the grisly scene. Floyd and his companions were immediately arrested.

May 25, 1930

"You were lucky," said a deputy sleepily. "Getting off for only doing the bank job in Sylvania."

"Yeah, lucky," replied Floyd quietly. Bradley had gotten the electric chair for killing Officer Manes. Atkins got life in prison. Floyd had been cleared of the murder charge, but convicted of bank robbery. Now, escorted by two deputies, he was on board a train speeding him to 15 years in the Ohio State Penitentiary. He had been in prison before and had vowed never to return again.

Floyd sat next to the window, his mind working fast and furiously as the wind blew across his face. The scenery flashed by at high speed. Floyd glanced over at the two deputies sleeping next to him. Suddenly, he made up his mind. In one swift movement, he was up and through the open window. Before the deputies knew what was happening, the bank robber was gone.

Gangsters preferred the V-8 because of it's roominess and speed.

"Stop the train!" yelled one deputy, now instantly awake. Running forward towards the locomotive, he yelled to the engineer, "Stop! Floyd's escaped!"

The other deputy watched from the train as the 29-year-old Floyd hit the ground next to the tracks and rolled down a hill. As if made of rubber, Floyd bounced up and starting running through a nearby cornfield.

"I did it!" laughed Floyd to himself. Glancing over his shoulder, he saw the train slowing down far in the distance. Over half a mile away, he kept running with no thought of stopping. "I said I wasn't going back to prison, and I'm not!" panted the escaped prisoner.

He never did go to prison, but he never stopped running either. The gangster was now doomed to a fate of his own choosing.

CHAPTER 1 — FLOYD'S YOUTH

Born in 1901 in the tiny town of Akins, Oklahoma, Charles Arthur Floyd grew up on his parents' farm in the nearby Cookson Hills. The Floyds slaved over the land, trying to bring in enough crops to feed the family. It was back-breaking work, but Charlie worked hard and didn't complain. However, the farm yielded little. Overworked, with little or no rain, this area in Oklahoma was growing into what became known in the 1930s as the Great Dust Bowl. The wind picked up the dry dirt, blowing it eastwardly across the country.

The black-haired, brown-eyed Floyd grew tall and muscular. He had little schooling, spending most of his youth working on his father's farm. Still, like other boys, he loved going into town and having a good time. His favorite drink was a local brew called Choctaw Beer. Soon many of his friends called him "Chock."

However, another name came to replace the gentlemanly "Charles Arthur" and fun-loving "Chock." Always carrying around a comb to keep his greased hair neatly in place, Charlie was teased by the locals as a "Pretty Boy." Floyd

In Oklahoma the drought of the 1930s caused the "Great Dust Bowl."

hated this nickname, but several women he knew started calling him "Pretty Boy" too, and the name stuck.

In 1924, Floyd married 16-year-old Wilma Hargrow. By the following year they found out she was going to have a baby. Floyd was pressed to find work to support his family. He took to the road, travelling from farm to farm, helping with harvests. The work was hard, the pay little. As the days passed, the young father-to-be grew more and more angry. He was willing to work, but there were no jobs to be had. One day he decided enough was enough.

"I know how to get some money," growled Floyd to a drifter sitting next to him at a hobo camp, where he was sleeping for the night.

"How?" asked the man. "There are no jobs anywhere in the state."

"No jobs, but there's money in those banks. Rich bankers taking over other peoples' farms. Well, I've worked hard and that money's due me," said Floyd angrily. "And I'm going into town and get some!"

"Good luck," replied the drifter, sleepily. "You'll be in jail before you can spend it."

If only Floyd had known how right the hobo was.

CHAPTER 2 — ROBBERY

It was late summer 1925, when Floyd bought a gun and sneaked on board the next train headed for St. Louis, Missouri. His timing was right, for just after he got into town, he pulled a payroll robbery, racing away with $5,000. It was more money than he'd ever had before.

Excitedly, he fled back to Oklahoma to see his young wife. For a few weeks the couple lived a life of luxury, spending the stolen money freely. However, on September 16, 1925 it all ended. Having traced the money to Floyd's home, Missouri police arrived and arrested the not-so-smart bank robber. In December, he was tried and found guilty of highway robbery. He spent the next three years in the Jefferson City State Penitentiary, during which time his son, Jack Dempsey Floyd, was born.

On March 7, 1929, Pretty Boy Floyd emerged, older and tougher from the Jefferson City Big House. His years inside had been filled with hard work and lashings. Looking up into the Missouri spring sky, he vowed fiercely to himself, "I'll never see the inside of a prison again!"

State Penitentiary where hardened criminals served time.

Over the next months, Floyd was arrested several times. Although suspected of robbery, he was never found guilty. He did, however, find himself in a court room, once again.

Returning to his home in Cookson Hills, Oklahoma, the 29-year-old Chock learned that his father had been gunned down by a Kentuckian, Jim Mills. It was an old feud between the two families. Although arrested and put on trial, Mills was found not guilty — he walked out of the court a free man. Floyd headed home, loaded his rifle, and followed Mills into the depths of Cookson Hills. Although no one knows what went on in those empty grasslands, the man who had killed Chock's father was never seen again. The people of Akins believed that "Chock done what he had to."

The following year, 1930, brought Floyd closer and closer to his role as a gangster. Teaming up with whatever low-lifes he could make contact with, he continued hitting banks and making payroll robberies. However, in March he was caught for robbing the Sylvania, Ohio bank. This time, he was sentenced to 10 to 25 years in prison. But Chock had no intention of serving any time. Ten miles from the Ohio State Pen, Floyd leaped out of the train's open window and high-tailed it across a corn field. He escaped, but he was running towards his own doom.

CHAPTER 3 — ON THE RUN

Heading for Toledo, Ohio, Floyd teamed up with Bill "The Killer" Miller. Miller, although four years Floyd's junior, had already killed five people, and set out to train the sure-shot Floyd to kill just as well.

The two headed into Michigan, where they pulled off many small robberies. Hitting gas stations and lone farmers, the two walked away with only a couple hundred dollars from each job. Still, after so many hits, they managed to build up a sizable stash, and fled to Kansas City to hide out.

In the safety of Mother Ash's lawless hotel, the robbery team met the woman's two sons, William and Wallace Ash and their wives, Rose and Beulah Baird, who were sisters. Floyd thought Rose was lovely, and Miller found Beulah wonderful. The two bank robbers killed the two

Ash brothers and raced away with their now-widowed wives.

Heading into Kentucky with the girls, Floyd and Miller continued their spree of bank robberies. There was $4,000 from the Mount Zion Trust Company, then $2,700 from the Elliston, Kentucky bank, onto Whitehouse, Kentucky, where they made off with $3,600. But their luck ran out in Bowling Green, Ohio.

"Do you know anything about the strangers that just came into town?" asked Police Chief Carl Galliher to Officer Ralph Castner.

"Nope," replied Castner. "What's the problem?"

"I've just got a feeling," answered Galliher suspiciously. "I'm gonna get those license plates checked out."

The police chief got the answer he expected —the car was stolen.

Driving into town, Miller and the two women were about to enter a store, while Floyd kept watch across the street.

"Hold on there," shouted Galliher, walking towards the trio.

Charles "Pretty Boy" Floyd.

"Duck, Bill!" screamed Floyd from across the street. Miller hit the floor immediately. From across the street, Floyd held a pistol in each hand and starting firing. His aim was good. Officer Castner crumpled in a bloody heap, killed instantly. Galliher raced for cover behind a nearby car.

While Galliher was moving, Miller took his chance. Jumping up, he ran towards his partner. The Police Chief was too quick and too good a shot to let "The Killer" get away. With fast, careful aim, Galliher fired. The shot hit Miller in the neck, nearly taking off his head. Reaching up towards his wound, Miller spun around, and then dropped to the ground dead.

Screaming, Beulah watched Miller fall. Without stopping to think, she raced for his gun and pointed it at her man's killer. Galliher was quicker. Again he aimed, and again his target dropped. Beulah was wounded, a bullet grazing her head.

Floyd watched as Rose was also wounded. He knew he had to make his move or join his dead companion. Like a Wild West outlaw, Floyd jumped up, legs apart, guns blazing. He saw his chance, and turned to race for the gang's stolen car. The engine roared to life as he turned the key. Only split seconds passed as the robber-turned-killer thundered down the street, foot pressing the gas pedal to the floor.

With this escape, Floyd's reputation grew. When reporters interviewed Madame Ash, whose two sons had been slayed for their wives, she asked,"Did they get "Pretty Boy?" No, but the newsmen picked up the hated nickname and spread it across the country.

CHAPTER 4 — A HOOD

Floyd took on a new partner, 40-year-old George Birdwell, a one-time preacher turned criminal, and continued hitting banks. The two created a crime spree unequaled in the southwestern United States. On December 12, 1931, they even managed to hit two banks on the same day. Now, however, the jobs were often violent, with many unfortunate victims falling prey to Floyd's skilled gunplay.

Strangely enough, Floyd became a hero in his home town in Oklahoma. Friends blamed the killings on Birdwell, and went on to weave stories

The inside of one of the many banks Floyd robbed.

on some of Floyd's "kindnesses." Acting like a Depression-days Robin Hood, Floyd took great pleasure in throwing some of his stolen loot to people on the street. Also, the seasoned robber often searched the bank presidents' desks to find mortgages. These loans, he hoped, hadn't been recorded. Happily, he ripped the legal papers into small pieces. Maybe, with his help, a few lucky people would never have to worry about losing their homes or farms to banks when they couldn't make the mortgage payment.

The bold robber wasn't above taking on his own town, even with all their praise of him. "I'm coming to see my mother," wrote Floyd to the sheriff in the nearby town of Sallisaw. "If you're smart you won't try to stop me." The sheriff had certainly heard of Floyd's skill with a gun, and wisely let the visit go unhindered.

Later, on a dare, Floyd drove boldly into town. Stopping his car outside the local barber shop, he waved to a couple of old friends.

"How de, Chock. What you doin' in town?" asked one.

"Going to rob the bank, Newt," replied Floyd with a smile. He did. It was this bold, foolish man who would soon go on to the big time, becoming America's Most Wanted.

CHAPTER 5 — KANSAS CITY MASSACRE

Floyd robbed so many banks that the governor of Oklahoma sent out a message to the people of the state, offering a $6,000 reward for Pretty Boy's capture, dead or alive.

The pretend Robin Hood heard the governor's statement and angrily sought to defend himself. Writing to a couple of detectives whom Floyd knew were searching for him, he stated, "I have robbed no one but moneyed men."

Still, with a price on his head, and his partner, Birdwell, killed in a bank robbery, Floyd left Oklahoma, heading eastward back to Kansas City, Missouri. It was here that his most notorious and most denied crime would take place.

On the summer morning of June 17, 1933, killer Frank Nash was being escorted by four police officers from the Union Railway Station in Kansas City. Nash had escaped from Kansas' Leavenworth State Penitentiary on October 19, 1930. That following year, while himself still hiding from the law, Nash had helped seven other

MOST WANTED
DEAD or ALIVE

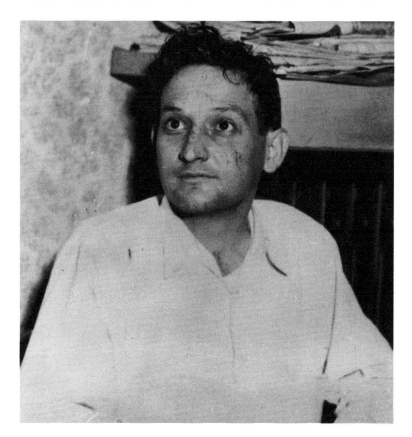

$6000.⁰⁰ REWARD

Leavenworth prisoners escape. Now, almost three years later, he had finally been recaptured. Nash's outlaw friends were determined to help him get away once again.

FBI Agents Frank Smith and F. Joseph Lackey, together with Police Chief Otto Reed, arrived by train with their prisoner early in the morning. FBI Special Agent R.E. Vetterli of the Kansas City Office, together with Agent R.J. Caffrey and Kansas City Police Officers W.J. Grooms and Frank Hermanson met them at the station.

"Everything looks OK," said Lackey to Vetterli, eyeing the train station carefully.

"Bring him out," said Vetterli.

The group of four FBI agents and three policemen circled Nash, moving him through Union Station's lobby and outside to Agent Caffrey's Chevrolet sedan. The doors were unlocked, and Nash was pushed into the front seat. As the agents were taking their places in the car, Lackey saw three men running from behind a car parked only six feet away from the Chevrolet. They were armed!

Lackey opened his mouth to shout a warning, but before he could make a sound, one of the gunmen shouted, "Up, up, up!"

Fort Leavenworth

Nash's friends had come to spring him. Suddenly, another voice yelled from his hiding place, "Let 'em have it!"

Gunfire echoed around the car. Officers Grooms and Hermanson died instantly. Special Agent Vetterli was shot in the arm but scrambled to hide behind the car just in time to see Agent Caffrey shot in the head. Agents Lackey and Smith, with Police Chief Reed, dropped low from their seats in the back of the car. Lackey took three bullets, but survived. Police Chief Reed was killed. Smith, in the middle, came out without a scratch. However, Nash himself was not as lucky. The murderer, sitting in the front seat, was riddled with bullets. He would never escape, nor kill, again.

Silence filled the air as gunmen hurried toward the Chevrolet. "They're all dead," said one.

"Let's get out of here," said another, turning to run.

As the three raced away, a Kansas City policeman, having heard the gunfire, emerged from Union Station and began shooting at the escaping killers. He hit one. The man stumbled, then kept running, leaping into a nearby car. "It was Pretty Boy Floyd," thought the officer as he watched the men speed off.

The attack lasted only 30 seconds. The three survivors identified the killers as one-time sheriff-turned-outlaw Vernon C. Miller, 23-year-old bank robber Adam Richetti, and escaped prisoner Charles Arthur "Pretty Boy" Floyd.

Floyd fiercely denied having had any part in the Kansas City Massacre. However, the FBI, Kansas City Police, and newspapers across the country blamed the known killer, making him Public Enemy Number One.

CHAPTER 6 — TO LIVE AND DIE

After the Kansas City tragedy, Floyd had only a little over a year to live. Floyd and Richetti joined up with the two Baird sisters, Rose and Beulah, and spent some time in New York. The four decided to return to Oklahoma.

Their trip began on October 20, with Floyd driving. Only a few hours later, near Wellsville, Ohio, he lost control of the car, and skidded into a telephone pole. It was a mistake that would later cost him his life.

FBI agent - Melvin Purvis.

While the two women drove the damaged car into Wellsville for repairs, Floyd and Richetti took their weapons and hid in some nearby woods. Police Chief J.H. Fultz was given several reports of two suspicious-looking men seen on the outskirts of town. Checking out the reports, Fultz discovered the two. On seeing the police chief, the gangsters immediately opened fire. Fultz was prepared, and captured Richetti, although the slippery Floyd managed to escape once again.

To get Floyd, FBI Agent Melvin Purvis, the man who had successfully tracked down bank robber John Dillinger only three months earlier, was called in. Purvis took over the manhunt, ordering local police to seal off the area.

On October 22, 1934, the law caught up with Public Enemy Number One. A car with Purvis and three other FBI agents patrolled the area together with another car of local police. From one of the roads near East Liverpool, Ohio, they saw an automobile move from behind a corn crib on a farm. They had been questioning people all along this area, looking for clues to Floyd's whereabouts. They stopped, deciding to talk with the driver of this car. The car pulled back behind

J. Edgar Hoover, extends his hand in congratulation to FBI agent Melvin Purvis.

the corn crib and out stepped their man! Floyd ran off, zigzagging his way across the nearby cornfield, gun in hand.

"Halt!" yelled Purvis and several other officers. "Halt!"

Floyd continued his wild run. However, this time his hopes of escaping the law and their deadly guns were futile. Eight bullets hit the 6'2" muscular killer, bringing him down in the field.

Cautiously, Purvis led his group of officers toward the fallen robber. Still clutching his .45 automatic pistol in his right hand, Floyd turned toward the lawmen and stated simply, "I'm done for. You've hit me twice."

"Are you Pretty Boy Floyd?" asked Purvis, as officers pulled the .45 pistol from the criminal's hand, and another from his belt.

Gritting his teeth against the pain, he answered angrily, "I am Charles Arthur Floyd." He hated the "Pretty Boy" nickname.

"Were you at the Kansas City Massacre?" asked an officer.

"I didn't do it. I wasn't in on it," snapped the bullet-ridden Floyd, using all his strength to pull himself up to his elbow. Hurrying on, he put a question to the officers: "Who tipped you off? I'm Floyd all right. You've got me this time."

An ambulance was called, but Floyd died within 15 minutes of the shooting. The strong arm of the law reached out and ended the 33-year-old killer/bank robber's life in a final grisly showdown.

EPILOGUE

Floyd's wife and son lived off his reputation. Early in 1934, the young mother and her nine-year-old son traveled the country advertising a movie made about criminals, called *"Crime Doesn't Pay."*

FBI agents found Vernon Miller, the other gunman believed to be involved in the Kansas City Massacre, dead on November 29, 1933. Miller had killed the henchman of a New Jersey hoodlum. The gunman's death was believed to have been revenge for that earlier murder.

Rose and Beulah Baird, the two sisters who had accompanied Floyd and Richetti, heard about

Richetti's capture while still at the garage in Wellsville, Ohio. As soon as the car was fixed, the two high-tailed it out of town. They later showed up in Sallisaw, Oklahoma to attend Floyd's funeral. Their love and adventures were ended.

Upon his capture, Adam Richetti was returned to Kansas City, where he was found guilty for his part in the June 17, 1933 massacre. Although he requested and received a second trial, he was again found guilty. On October 7, 1938, he went to the gas chamber.

At the time Floyd was killed, a watch was found with ten notches etched on it. Supposedly, the killer had scratched these on to mark the death of each of his victims.

In the beginning, the man tried to live a life within the rules, but hard times led him to the easy-pickings of the criminal world. Like many others before him, he fought against the law and lost. Now he bears forever the black legend and despised nickname of Public Enemy Number One: "Pretty Boy" Floyd.